Self-Talk in the Garden:

A Collection of Mindful Poems

Self-Talk in the Garden:

A Collection of Mindful Poems

by

Christen A. Careaga

© 2025 Christen A. Careaga. All rights reserved.
This material may not be reproduced in any form, published,
reprinted, recorded, performed, broadcast,
rewritten or redistributed without
the explicit permission of Christen A. Careaga.
All such actions are strictly prohibited by law.

Cover design by Shay Culligan
Cover image by John Friedrick
Author photo by Ariel Careaga

ISBN: 978-1-63980-826-7

Kelsay Books
502 South 1040 East, A-119
American Fork, Utah 84003
Kelsaybooks.com

For Ariel, my muse.

"What you seek is seeking you."
—Rumi

Acknowledgments

Profound appreciation to the Kelsay Books team for so graciously giving me the opportunity to put this work out into the world.

Thanks so much to the following for making room for my poems—

Poetry of Presence II: More Mindfulness Poems, edited by Phyllis Cole-Dai and Ruby R. Wilson: "Forgiveness"
How to Love the World: Poems of Gratitude and Hope, edited by James Crews: "Shells"
Oregon East, edited by Christopher Densmore and Lora Alix: "Man on the Metro," "From Dust," "Self-Talk in the Garden," "Contentment"
Love Is for All of Us: Poems of Tenderness and Belonging from the LGBTQ+ Community and Friends, edited by James Crews and Brad Peacock: "Intimacy"

An abundance of thanks to my professor and mentor, James Crews, who helped me believe my voice was legitimate and worth listening to. Deepest gratitude to my sweet family, my first fans and biggest cheerleaders: Mom, Dad, Daniel, Micah, and Abby. All my heart of thanks to my husband Ariel Careaga, without whom none of this would have happened (and to our sweet Solomon, who joined us at the tail-end of this project). Last, thank you to the Creator—faith and connection to the Spirit are my truest sources of inspiration.

Contents

Reunion	11
What the River Carries	12
An Invitation	14
A Burning Bush	16
When Inspiration Comes	17
Turning Toward the Light	19
Communion	20
Hong Kong Lunch Hour	22
Lectio Divina on a Tuesday	24
God of the Rivers	25
Longlining for Halibut	27
The Long Cast	28
Forgiveness	30
Work	32
My Nature	34
From Dust	36
When My Mother Plays	38
Intimacy	40
Basking	41
Hearts	42
Thankful	43
Contentment	44
Everyday Things	45
Recovery	47
Rehab	48
Being Brave	49
Man on the Metro	51
Well-Being	53
Lentil Soup	54
Shells	55
Reconciling	56
Self-Talk in the Garden	58

Reunion

Sitting on the river's bank,
the pieces of you
that had been floating
without gravity,
drifting downstream,
land back in your body.

Mind fits back
inside skull.
Breath billows
back into lungs.
Beating heart lands
with a gentle thud
in your waiting chest.

Those parts find their way back to you,
and you wind them up gently,
this wayward ball of yarn
that became your life,
with its strings
loose in all directions.

What the River Carries

The river carries ducklings
on its back—born this spring
with tiny, webbed feet
and downy wings as
soft as cotton balls,
riding the water with
childlike faith.

On its back, the river carries
a skin of fallen leaves,
blinking golden amber,
newly shed from
oak and alder that
line its banks.

The river carries
you and me,
bobbing along
in a secondhand canoe, fragile
as a cork boat.

Ducklings will sprout
sleek, long feathers
and fly from river to wetland
and back, carrying in their bellies
the seeds for a new
riparian forest.

Leaves will catch in great clots,
trapped in branches of fallen logs,
wet and warm for
salmon eggs and beavers' paws
—still-water shelter for young fish,
the brick and mortar of a home.

And you and me?
What can we offer
this watery mother who
bears us on her shoulders?
How to repay so steep a debt?

An Invitation

Come, let's shed our skin a while.
Perhaps feathers feel lighter
than these bodies,
and when I look up
at the black-capped chickadee,
nipping, beak to breast,
tenderly on its soft little coat,
I think I'd like to try that too.

Come, let's let the human weight
drop at our ankles for a while.
What if, instead, we put on a cloak of bark,
grooved and ancient, sticky and soft
with moss and sap.
You'll love, too, the way
it gives and pushes back
against our palms,
the safety of a body like that.

Or what if we wore no skin at all?
Evaporating into mist,
into air,
just for a day?
Shifting from cloud
to rain and back.

That heaviness in the chest,
the way it contracts
in the first waking moment,
would that dissipate too, do you think?

And after all that,
when we slip back
into ourselves,
I'll recognize you still,
when the light
catches you just right,
the shimmer of a wing,
the heady scent of wood.

A Burning Bush

Outside my window:
a crabapple tree
brimming with birds.
You can't tell at first.

It's just branches and green leaves,
but then they start to move.
A scrub jay launches
from upper perch to lower
—a rush of blue-black feathers.
Chittering and multiplying,
a dozen chickadees trade
places with each other.
I don't know how I didn't see before;
the tree is alive with them.

This reminds me of the lavender
by my front door,
and how, yesterday, when pausing
a moment to find keys,
I heard a gentle murmuring,
only then finding honeybees
vibrating on stems and buds,
only then startled awake
by a holy bush on fire.

When Inspiration Comes

after Marjorie Saiser

It approaches like a long-legged,
slender animal in the brush,
shy and nearly invisible,
just a glimmer of fawn,
brown in between leaves.

You want to approach, catch
sight of the whole creature
and know that you didn't
just imagine it.

But you are scared to do anything
but peek out of the corner of your eye.
Otherwise, it will flee,
like a word on the tip of your tongue,
or your mother's house cat, vanishing
whenever sought,
whenever wanted.

It is not always like this.
There have been days
when Inspiration frightened you
with its boldness,
a fire you kindled
and coaxed and loved
until it lit, then broke
beyond the limits
of your hearth
onto anything moving

nearby: tree limbs,
woven rugs, the edges of your sweater.
A hunger like that
could eat up a whole life.

Turning Toward the Light

Forgive me:
When you tapped on my windowpane,
your breath fogging it, warm and alive,
when you asked if I'd come
outside into the wonder,
I ignored and walked into
the kitchen for a sandwich instead.
Forgive me:
When I was driving and a scattering flock
of blackbirds rose from the corn
like a miracle,
I only noticed for a moment
before rehearsing the day's tasks again,
gripping the steering wheel,
white-knuckled once more.

The gift, though, is this
—you don't hold a grudge.
Instead, you patiently wait
for my face to turn
toward you, toward the light, again,
as you know it will.

Communion

You sip morning air
like communion wine,
letting the rich, earthy
body of it fill you.

But the world is already awake:
the belch of the garbage truck
rattles you.
High voices of first-graders
en route to class
grate at your nerves.
You see your neighbor
crossing to your porch,
and you know she wants to talk
about her 40-year-old son
who refuses to move out.

And you sigh heavy,
the rich morning
growing sour in your mouth.

You think about switching towns,
changing lives,
simply pretending
you didn't see your neighbor
and retreating inside
when something stops you.

It is the same voice
that's given you pause other times,
quiet, strong, insistent
—ready to be listened to
if you are even just a little bit willing.
The voice that's led you back to loving
more than once.

You lift your hand slowly to wave,
easing into this greeting
as you would wade
into the shallow end of the pool,
as if you are bringing the cup of life
back up to your lips.

Hong Kong Lunch Hour

In the close-cornered dim sum restaurant
a cart emerges, loaded with
tall, gleaming tins—stacks
of steaming pork and shrimp buns
nestled inside like eggs in a nest.

They appear
like communion trays
stacked on themselves at the church altar,
papery wafers and little beakers
of bargain grape juice tucked within.
Back then, hunger at the noon-hour
close of service would clench
the stomach like a fist,
that unique, fierce hunger
only children know:

the body and the blood
of Christ in those tasteless wafers,
like tissue on the tongue.

Even so, at the sight of dim sum,
the heart swells and the head becomes dizzy,
as with warm wine;
almost seven thousand miles of ocean
stretch between back then and now,
but perhaps this is how God feels.

Outside of you and then suddenly inside,
molecule by molecule,
becoming you.
The waiter lifts the lid.
All you see is steam.

Lectio Divina on a Tuesday

Can it be a prayer,
the way I fold
a work shirt for my love,
tucking it right at the seam
to avoid wrinkles?

Can it be a prayer,
the weightless joy I feel
watching a squirrel
mouth an entire apple
just fallen from its tree?

Is it sacred when
I make eye contact
with the man at the stop sign
asking for cash,
even though I want
to fiddle with the radio knob instead?

Today, these,
my small offerings
in an expanding universe.

God of the Rivers

A sparkling God
that I see for an instant
—the silver flash of scales
vanish into cold depths.

God of the beasts,
hidden behind the brush with
yellow glowing eyes
that could eat a man alive.

God of the rocks.
A heavy God
cascading in landslides
with the strength
to carry on his back
the foundation of a city, the bedrock,
the weight of a human life.

Where are you now?
In the cosmic quiet of the moon,
the wide silence of the sky?

God of newborn baby fingernails,
of every mother holding her child
close to her breast.
God of every grandfather lonely in bed
with soft, wrinkled head on cool pillow.

Where are you now?

I catch your shadow sometimes
or see your shape behind the brush,
feel the prickle on my skin
and know I'm not alone.

Longlining for Halibut

Thrashing,
a flash of metallic scales
on the floor of the skiff.

They catch the temporary sun,
and the light glints,
too, on the fish's fragile eye,
an amber marble
with dilated pupil,

life expanding the shining black
as it fights.

Its tail kicks
at anyone within range,
exposing back, belly,
sleek and vulnerable,
and I see its gills
—crimson and blossoming,
delicate as rose petals.

When we are home,
safe down south in the lower 48,
the halibut lies in packages
in my freezer, cold, pale,
unmoving.

Packages my mother will give to her neighbor.
Packages my husband will give to his boss.
Given and received
until all the life is shared among us.

The Long Cast

If I cast my mind back
like I would a fishing line,
whizzing and zinging
through the air,
feather lure bristling
in the wind,
it might land
in the front yard of Marshall Drive
with nine-year-old me
breathing in air
redolent with magnolias.
The cast may land
in the old family van
where I am 15, hands
white and gripping
the steering wheel
for the first time,
the neighborhood roads too small
for me to drive between the lines.
On the gentle, lapping water,
bobbing now,
my long cast may land
in an autumn evening,
night college classes
and the sunset pulling
maple tree shadows
long across quiet streets.

I pull; I start to reel in
the line I threw.
It hooks and snags
on anything it can find
along the way home:
the yeasty, golden scent of neighborhood bakery,
the wild, too-big pain of first bone break.

And when my mind
finally returns
in a mess of pondweeds
and crushed aluminum cans,
I will pick through all this debris
and treasure,
tending and untangling
memories with gentle fingers.

Forgiveness

after Lynn Ungar

One morning,
I'll wake up to find
I'm not mad anymore.
That the anger I'd stoked
and attended to like a fire,
like a flame my life depended on,
isn't necessary.

As early sun enters my room
with streamers of light,
I'll be surprised to find
I have forgiven you.

The tender part of me you hurt,
maybe hurt without realizing,
is not so inflamed.
It used to throb
like splinter under skin,
red and unavoidable.

And now, this daybreak
seems to have worked
it out of me.
I didn't even notice.

The body has a way of doing that
if we just step aside.

When I think of you that morning,
it will be with only good wishes,
recalling how kind you are,
how brilliant,
how full of promise.

I will see clearly then.

Work

Like shoveling snow,
this forgiveness business
—heavier and harder
than it first appears.

Offense arrives quietly, sometimes,
and when it's cold enough
it sticks, and stacks.

This growing weight
can cave in a roof
or snap the limbs
of our ancient sequoia.
It could kill me,
but I don't always notice.

This morning I do.
Now, I'm out, up to my knees, working
with hands, elbows, shoulders,
trying to keep the thought
from my head:
It will snow again tonight,
and undo all the progress
I have made.

Even so,
shiny shovel tip under snow pile,
I will lift,
and continue lifting,
muscles singing, alive.

My Nature

Inside me,
trees were planted long ago,
and a wood now stands
pleasant and dappled
with buttery light,
enough shade to grow sleepy under,
enough trunks to lean a weary spine against.
When inside my wood, I often forget
the planet beyond it keeps moving.
I could get lost in here, and do,
looping around thoughts and feelings
that took root years back,
old seeds dropped in old, needled ground.

Rivers course through
my insides too,
clear, constantly moving.
On a summer day, this river
looks like a friend, carrying
slippery fat rainbow trout and water skippers, too.
Other times of year, though,
the water turns blue-black,
and when I stick my hand in its depths,
the bones in my fingers ache right down to the marrow.
I wade up to my knees anyway.

Inside me
are high dunes of curving red sand
and in other parts, miles
of sagebrush, thirsty and prickled.

It takes time to cross my deserts,
these neglected patches,
overlooked and considered dangerous.
But catch me at the edge of nightfall,
and my rabid energy will seem soft,
even feminine, in deep plum and saffron;
it is that dusky time
when jackrabbit and fennec fox appear,
sniffing the air gently to make sure all is safe.

From Dust

Maybe life is about returning.
Maybe it's a constant practice
in tracing our own footprints.

We miss the water of mother's womb
and find our way back,
dropping ourselves inside
oceans, rivers,
into hot, blessed baths.

Or maybe it's just our mother we miss.

Remember the warmth
radiating from her skin,
the familiar scent of safety.

After those early days,
our fingers
discover their match in another's hands.
The boundaries of our own skin
dissolve into a lover's.
Wedding rings, friendship bracelets . . .
Lock yourself to me and don't leave,
we say.

But think of all the ways we separate too:
shoes that keep feet
from the feel of grass;
houses that wall us from each other
and from the air that embraces everything.

In spite of all this,
the world keeps trying.

And, sometimes,
the dust of your skin and mine
swirls and swoops,
merging in a bar of afternoon light.

When My Mother Plays

The piano was my grandfather's last gift.
It was the only thing
Mom bought with her inheritance,
and now it takes up
a whole room:

quiet, shining, dark,
with an outstretched row
of sparkling keys.

Don't forget to pull the shade,
my mother gently reminds
when new sun burns the piano's wood
or cold air leaks through the windowpanes.

The room has become a kind of church,
and I'll sit there alone sometimes,
especially when I am homesick
for things I can't put into words.

When she slides onto the bench,
when her long, strong fingers
rest on keys,
I can see her at fifteen
practicing four hours a day,
dreams of becoming
a concert pianist
in her young head.

She leans into the grand as though
she has become one of the vibrating strings,
as if her neck, shoulders, rib cage
have all been struck like a bell,
and now she resounds,
each bone humming in response.

Intimacy

It is the bee
dipping itself into the slender cup
of a morning glory,
one hidden inside the other.
It is the way water
gentles its body against riverbank.
It is the hawk hugging itself
into wind,
current holding bird like a hand.
It is the expression on your face when
you first noticed me,
before I knew your touch like my own.
The day your eyes took me in
like a shelter,
loving before even knowing why.

Basking

Cup a rose
in your hand.
Tilt it toward you,
but gently,
like you would
the face of a dear child
or true love,
a slow and tender enough
touch so as not to lose
any petals,
so as not to control
or damage. You just want
to catch its presence,
to be blessed for that moment
inside the world it creates.

Hearts

after Danusha Lameris

Are glorious kites,
catching and climbing
a blustery gale.
Are sticks of dynamite
chock full of color.
Volumes of love poems
begun in elementary school.
Ropes we throw out
to a gasping friend.
Ropes we throw out
to ourselves.

Thankful

Clean paper sheet and fingertips across it.
Clean bed sheets, cool on bare skin.
Wet, clean hair tied high in a knot.
Tall piles of April clouds, plates of creamed potatoes.
Folds of storm clouds—purple and black.
Dog-eared pages, deep memory creases.
Dog curled into himself, nose tucked into couch cushion.
Me curled into you—safe under your chin.

Contentment

Does caring mean collapsing
into something?
For I know how to collapse:
how to fall into
a job, an idea, a person,
and let that gravity command my orbit.

There is a drunken magic to it,
and I remember every time
the body of myself
has been possessed.

But there is something, too,
to this Sunday afternoon
when somehow, I have detached
from all my lovely
obsessions, and now my chest moves
up and down with breath,
unburdened.

The way the light falls
on young grass,
new and pale this early spring,
that is enough for now.

Everyday Things

Some things lie lonely
when not in use:
mud boots in dark closets,
fire pokers by ashy furnace,
wine glasses nestled against
each other's chilly glass skin.

But they speak of what we are to each other—
The year I quit my job
without finding another first,
you were unwavering and waterproof,
covering my steps in the midst
of all I would wade through.

The year your school shut down
and the old depression reared
its broken-toothed face,
I tried to prod you,
move you gently enough
to keep your coals warm
and remind you
you're still alive.

And the year we began worrying
over our aging parents
(that strange reversal they said would happen),
when we struggled to protect
their immune systems from
nightmares on the news,

we became containers of hope
for each other,
something, even something small,
that could hold a sparkle of beating,
twinkling joy,
could go down into our spirits
and stave off the cold.

Recovery

I watch a seagull
right before takeoff,
the sandbelt
his stretch of runway.

The air isn't lifting him
at first.
At the start,
he is just
legs and feet and body.

But then, the moment comes;
his arms stretch
into wings,
and the cold breeze coming off the water,
the same one hitting my numb face,
swoops under him.
He is airborne.

Beloved:
so, too, with you.
You will not always be
weighed down.
The moment will come
when you remember
you have wings.

Rehab

A great drop,
that's what it's like
for a colt
in their first moments.
They move from
the familiar, enclosed space
that became their home
to something new and bright
and cold, and they land hard,
no cushion in the space
between Mother and Earth.
Legs don't work yet.
They feel too spindly,
too thin and stick-like
to support weight,
but they will;
they do.

Being Brave

In Paris, I wanted to cut my hair.
Shear it clear to the sharp
edge of my chin
—the first time since I was a girl.

I wanted to cut off the past year
of split ends and dead ends,
of done friendships,
and coming to the end of myself.

Walking the narrow, warm alleys
between *Rue Moliere* and *Rue de Rivoli,*
the weight of all that hung
on my shoulders like a prison.

But I was afraid in Paris
and passed the salon
three times,
anxious of the woman
I would become.

I had to wait instead
until I was in front of my mirror
back home,
alone with the scissors
in my own hands.

With clean, swift snips,
pieces, soft and brown,

were swirling down the sink.

In a quiet space
that belonged to me,
I could be brave.

Man on the Metro

We become children
when we sleep.

At first, I thought it was only you,
with your Peter Pan face and eyelashes
fluttering with dreams,
but today, the man on the metro was a child too.

His unshaved jaw,
the purple circles
like bruises under his eyes,
all dissolve with the rhythmic
little-boy breath,
all melt with the up
and the down of his ribcage
—a breath like a bird inside
trying to break free.

A head of unkempt, dark hair,
the same hair his mother ruffled softly
before bedtime,
drops heavy on one shoulder.

In moments like this,
all the growing up years,
those decades trying to succeed as *adult,*

even the responsibilities waiting
on the other end of the rail line,
seem to ebb
and, to our great relief,
fade softly away.

Well-Being

On harder days, when
getting out of bed
feels like climbing out of a pit,
remember other times
when it's been different.
Mornings when your eyes open,
and you realize with relief
it's an unexpected snow day,
or times a phone chime rouses you,
and it is the little sister
you've been worried about,
finally responding;
you let go of a deep worry breath
you didn't realize you were holding.
This is the same feeling
as when a mother or father says,
"Everything will be okay,"
and you believe them, really.
The same warmth fills you
when all the people you love most
are under the same roof,
and it starts to rain, tapping
against the shingles
—a friendly voice whispering,
You are safe, you are safe, you are safe.

You might not feel all that
this morning,
but you will again soon.

Lentil Soup

Cooking is like breathing.

Sometimes, I forget to inhale
until the serrated blade
cuts down into yellow onion
or into the wet and cold carrots.

How strange, too, the way
running fingers through
tall jars of rice and lentils
lowers the blood pressure;
the way water running
through grains and legumes,
rinsing off outer husks and grit,
slows my too-fast pace.

At first, the faucet's stream
comes through the strainer
milky with extra starch.
But if I keep letting it run,
keep letting it spill over,
constant and steady,
soon, water will pour clear,
sparkling through lentils and jasmine rice.

Shells

The curl of your ear,
a tiny pearl of a shell
that I kiss so gently
you can barely feel it,
barely hear it.

That pink flushing hot
with sleep,
nape of your neck damp,
as I tuck the blankets too tight.

Remember when you were three
and held one to your face?
Was it a cockle shell, a conch shell?
Some polished swirl of light.

Wet sand on cheek,
you listened

like I listen,
to make sure you are
still breathing,
watching for that
tiny throb of life
pressing at your throat.

Reconciling

Gravity gains momentum
even as we lose ours,
like a backward childhood.

When we are young,
we are filled with helium,
lifted off our feet
by some floating volition
tied to our ankles.
It carries us into tree limbs
and handstands.

Sometimes, back then,
the low gravity would cause us
to bounce on our heels
or school desks;
it got us into trouble
now and again.

But along the way,
things switched.
When it hit me,
I woke up
and instead of air
lifting me out of bed,
I had to fight,
to swim through molecules,
suddenly become
viscous as mud.

And driving this afternoon,
I see it, too
—a man bent in half,
gravity riding his back like a king,
it has grown so fat
and vigorous.

Is this why we feel the urge
to travel into space or out to sea?
For some relief?

Water buoys us up;
the night sky carries our weight.

I want to befriend gravity,
to stop seeing this as a war
I am not winning,
and instead,
lean into
this new groundedness.

To lie, back flat
on this unmown
backyard patch,
and embrace
the way my spine
curves into the soil,
the way the Earth holds us.

Self-Talk in the Garden

Be gentle with your garden plot.
Take care which seeds you choose to plant,
and when you decide, tuck them
into earth with faith they'll thrive.

Water graciously.
It is not a waste;
you are not a waste.

When those weeds spring up eager heads,
take a moment to see if it's invasive
or just a medicinal dandelion.
And if it *is* something that will choke,
like unforgiveness,
dig deep but be gentle at finding the root.
If it grows back in the same spot
(as it will), don't give up.
It takes time to clear your ground.

Sometimes, just plunge your hands
into your land and delight
in its dark, spicy richness,
with all its pebbles and twigs
and earthworms.

Let the world come rest here
—the pill bug with its shiny exoskeleton,
the dragonfly with shimmering shadow wings.

If it's noisy and messy,
all the better.

Remember,
when you are waiting,
some bulbs rest all winter,
but that doesn't mean they're dead
or that you are a failure.
Your garden
will surprise you one day.

You'll walk out your door
and find the soft, young leaves
of cornflower, of poppy
—shy and beautiful,
happy to see sun for the first time.

About the Author

Christen Careaga, a native of Oregon's Willamette Valley, is a longtime educator who loves seeing children, teens, and adults fall in love with writing for the first time. She likes to spend her days with her husband and their little son, Solomon.

www.ingramcontent.com/pod-product-compliance
Lightning Source LLC
Chambersburg PA
CBHW030915170426

43193CB00009BA/854